GREAT RECORD BREAKERS IN SPORTS™

WAYNE GRETZKY
HOCKEY ALL-STAR

Rob Kirkpatrick

The Rosen Publishing Group's
PowerKids Press™
New York

To John Elway, the Wayne Gretzky of quarterbacks.

Published in 2001 by The Rosen Publishing Group, Inc.
29 East 21st Street, New York, NY 10010

First Edition

Book Design: Michael de Guzman

Photo Credits: p. 4 © Al Bello/Allsport; p. 7 © Mike Powell/Allsport and © CORBIS/Bettmann; p. 8 © The Globe and Mail, Toronto, Canada; p. 11 © Canapress Photo Service; p. 12 CORBIS/Neal Preston; p. 15 © Allsport; p. 16 © Tim de Frisco/Allsport and © Allsport; p. 19 © Allsport; p. 20 © Rick Stewart/Allsport; p. 22 © Ezra Shaw/Allsport.

Kirkpatrick, Rob.
    Wayne Gretzky, hockey all-star / by Rob Kirkpatrick.
        p. cm.—(Great record breakers in sports)
    Includes index.
    ISBN 0-8239-5631-8 (lib. bdg.)
    1. Gretzky, Wayne, 1961—Juvenile literature. 2. Hockey players—Canada—Biography—Juvenile literature.
I. Title. II. Series.

GV848.5.G73 K57 2000
796.962'092—dc21
[B]   99-048080

Manufactured in the United States of America

CONTENTS

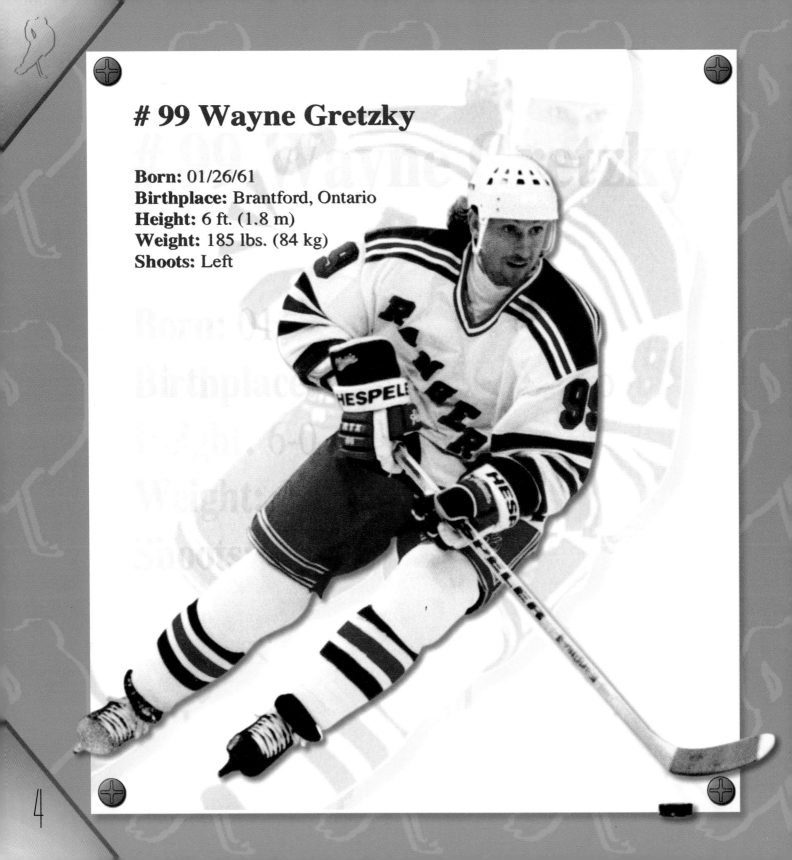

99 Wayne Gretzky

Born: 01/26/61
Birthplace: Brantford, Ontario
Height: 6 ft. (1.8 m)
Weight: 185 lbs. (84 kg)
Shoots: Left

MEET WAYNE GRETZKY

Did you ever see Wayne Gretzky play hockey? If you did, you probably saw him score a goal. Scoring a goal is hard to do, but Wayne made it look easy. He scored 894 goals over the 20 years he played in the **National Hockey League**, or NHL. To score a goal, a player has to **shoot** a **puck** past the other team's **goalie** and into that team's **net**, all while skating on ice. Wayne also knew how to help his teammates score goals. He assisted other players. This means that he made passes and helped teammates score. Wayne had 1,963 assists during his career. Wayne had more goals and more assists than any other player in NHL history.

◀ *Wayne Gretzky delighted hockey fans with his outstanding passing ability.*

RECORD KEEPING IN HOCKEY

The NHL was formed in 1917. Since then, the league has kept track of all the goals that have been scored and the players who scored them. One reason the league keeps these records is so that we can compare players like Wayne with players from the past. For instance, a player named Gordie Howe used to play for the Detroit Red Wings. Gordie set the record for most career goals (801), assists (1,049), and points (1,850). Points are the number of goals plus assists. These records lasted until Wayne broke all three of them. In fact, Wayne broke or tied 61 different NHL records during his career.

Wayne was playing for the Los Angeles Kings when he broke Gordie Howe's record for all-time leading scorer. ▶

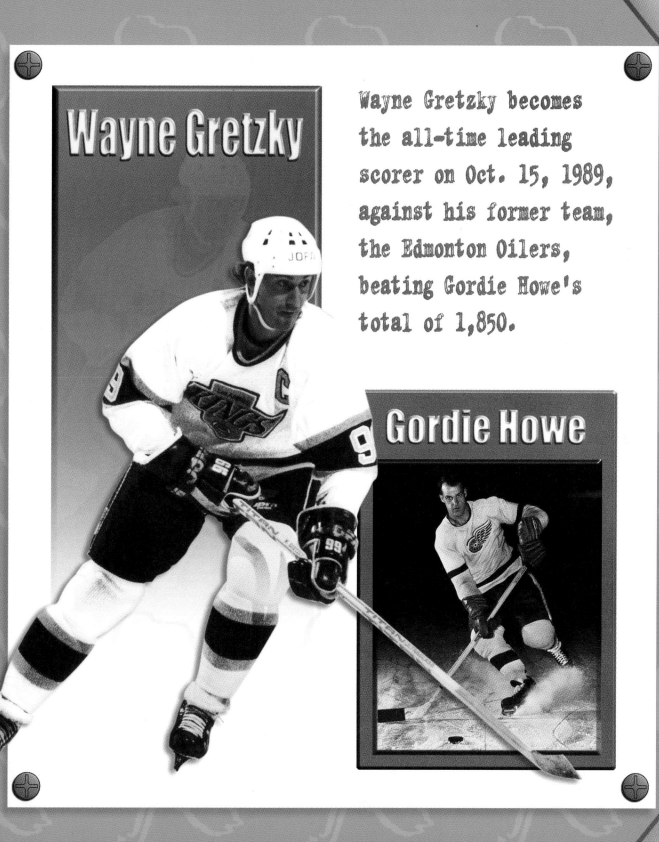

Wayne Gretzky

Wayne Gretzky becomes the all-time leading scorer on Oct. 15, 1989, against his former team, the Edmonton Oilers, beating Gordie Howe's total of 1,850.

Gordie Howe

THE GREAT ONE

Wayne started playing hockey when he was just two years old. He grew up in Brantford, a city in Ontario, Canada. When he was six, he began to play in the Brantford Atom League, which was mostly for 10-year-old players. Wayne played very well against these older players. When he was 10, Wayne scored 378 goals in only 68 games. This broke the old league record of 140 goals. A local newspaper writer started to call Wayne the Great One because he was such a good player. This nickname stuck with Wayne for the rest of his career.

◀ *When Wayne was 10 years old, he already had a hockey card. Even at this age, Wayne had broken a league record.*

WAYNE BECOMES AN OILER

In 1979, when Wayne was 18, he started playing in the NHL with the Edmonton Oilers. That season, he scored 51 goals in 79 games. The team had a lot of good young players, like Jari Kurri, Paul Coffey, and Mark Messier. Wayne enjoyed passing the puck to his teammates. He had 86 assists that year. When you add his goals and assists, he had 137 points. That means that Wayne either scored or helped his teammates score 137 goals in 79 games. He tied Marcel Dionne of the Los Angeles Kings for leading scorer in points. Marcel outscored Wayne, though, in total goals, 53 to 51, for the 1979–80 season.

In Wayne's first season with the Edmonton Oilers, he scored a total of 137 points. ▶

Wayne Gretzky's Rookie Stats:

Games Played	Goals	Assists	Points
79	51	86	137

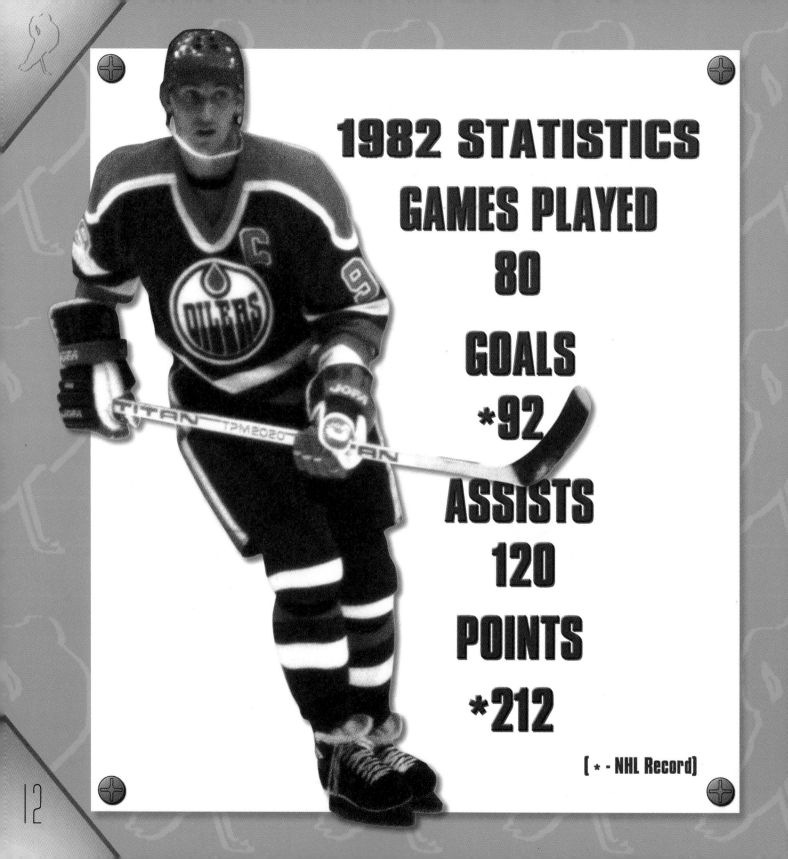

1982 STATISTICS

GAMES PLAYED
80

GOALS
*92

ASSISTS
120

POINTS
*212

(* - NHL Record)

WAYNE IS THE BEST IN THE NHL

In the early 1980s, many people believed that Wayne was the best player in hockey. In the 1981–82 season, he scored 212 points. That was a record because no one had ever scored more than 152 points in one season! He set another record by scoring 92 goals in that season. This record stands today. In 1983, his team, the Oilers, went to the **Stanley Cup finals**. The finals are the last games of the **playoffs**. The Oilers lost to the New York Islanders in the finals. Wayne ended the next season with 205 points. In the 1984 playoffs, the Oilers returned to the finals to play the Islanders again. This time the Oilers won the Stanley Cup!

◀ *Wayne broke the regular season scoring record of 152 points by ending the 1981–82 season with 212 points.*

WAYNE HELPS BUILD A DYNASTY

In the 1985 playoffs, Wayne made 47 points and set a record for the most points ever made in the playoffs. He also tied a record with seven goals in the finals, helping the Oilers beat the Philadelphia Flyers. Wayne broke his own single-season scoring record in 1986. He set a new all-time record of 215 points. In 1987, the Oilers went to the finals and beat the Philadelphia Flyers again. Then, in the 1988 Stanley Cup finals, they swept the Boston Bruins, four games to none. This means that the Oilers won all the games in the finals. Wayne set the finals record with 13 points. He had helped the Oilers build a **dynasty**.

Wayne helped lead the Oilers to four Stanley Cup victories. ▶

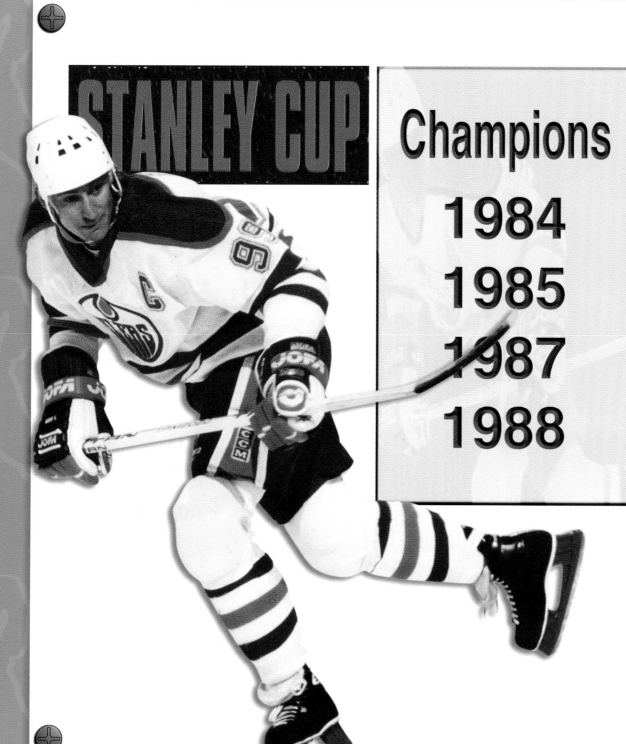

STANLEY CUP

Champions
1984
1985
1987
1988

In 1988, the Edmonton Oilers traded Wayne Gretzky to the Los Angeles Kings.

THE TRADE

By the end of the 1988 season, the Oilers had won four Stanley Cups in five years. Their fans were happy. Hockey fans were confused when Wayne was **traded** to the Los Angeles Kings. Fans did not understand why the Oilers traded Wayne. The reason was that Wayne's wife, Janet Jones, was an actress. She worked in Hollywood, California, and Wayne wanted to live with her. The Oilers did Wayne a favor because he had done so much for them. They moved him from Ontario, Canada, to Los Angeles, which is near Hollywood. Wayne was sad to leave his teammates on the Oilers, but he looked forward to starting a family with his wife.

◀ *Wayne's trade to the Los Angeles Kings made all the newspaper headlines. It was the most surprising trade in hockey history.*

WAYNE IN LOS ANGELES

The Kings were not a very good team when Wayne started playing for them. He helped them get better, though. In the 1989 playoffs, Wayne helped the Kings beat his old team, the Oilers. Wayne also kept breaking NHL records with the Kings. On October 15, 1989, Wayne broke the all-time record for points made in a career with his 1,851st point. More and more fans came to see the all-time point leader play in Los Angeles. In 1993, the Kings surprised their fans by going all the way to the Stanley Cup finals. They lost in the finals to the Montreal Canadiens. Fans were still pleased by how well Wayne had played.

Wayne met with the press after he broke the all-time record for points made in a career. His idol, Gordie Howe, joined him at the meeting. ▶

Oct. 15, 1989

POINT # 1,851
NHL Record

LOTS OF TEAMS WANT WAYNE

In 1996, the Kings decided they needed a change. They traded Wayne to the St. Louis Blues. This was the last year of Wayne's contract, though. This meant that he could leave the Blues when his contract was up. Then he could join any team that wanted him. The New York Rangers wanted Wayne to come play for them. Wayne signed a new contract with the Rangers in 1997. Ranger fans were thrilled to have the record-setting player in New York. They looked forward to watching Wayne fire the puck into the net in the Rangers' arena, or ice hockey rink, at Madison Square Garden.

◀ *In the 1996–97 season, his first season with the New York Rangers, Wayne scored 25 goals and 72 assists.*

WAYNE RETIRES ON TOP

Wayne brought excitement to the Rangers. He helped them beat the New Jersey Devils in the 1997 playoffs. In 1999, he had 62 points, more than anyone else on the Rangers. Although Wayne was still playing well, he decided it was time to **retire**. His last game was on April 18, 1999, in New York's Madison Square Garden against the Pittsburgh Penguins. The Penguins won in **overtime**, but the fans still cheered for Wayne because of his great career. The NHL retired his number. This means that no other player will ever wear number 99 on his shirt. People still call Wayne the Great One. Many people feel he was the best hockey player ever to play the game.

GLOSSARY

dynasty (DY-nas-tee) A team that has won many championships in a short period of time.

finals (FY-nulz) A series of games between the best two teams in the playoffs. The first team to win four games in the finals wins the Stanley Cup.

goalie (GOH-lee) The player who guards the net and tries to catch or block the other team's shots.

National Hockey League (NAH-shun-uhl HAH-kee LEEG) An organization of the best professional hockey teams in North America.

net (NET) The goal into which players try to shoot the puck.

overtime (OH-ver-tym) Extra time added onto a hockey game that has ended in a tie.

playoffs (PLAY-ofs) Games that the top teams from the season play in to compete for the Stanley Cup.

puck (PUHK) The hard and flat rubber disc used to score points in hockey.

retire (ree-TY-er) When a player decides not to play professionally anymore.

shoot (SHOOT) When a player hits the puck toward the other team's net with his stick.

Stanley Cup (STAN-lee KUHP) The NHL trophy awarded to the winner of the playoffs.

traded (TRAY-dehd) When a player is sent to another team in exchange for another player.

INDEX

WEB SITES

To learn more about Wayne Gretzky, check out these Web sites:

http://cbs.sportsline.com/u/hockey/nhl/players/19279.htm
http://www.cnnsi.com/gretzky